PERFECTION LEARNING®

Collecting and Sorting
Insects

Cathy Elliott

Table of Contents

About Insects

Imagine weighing every creature on Earth together on one huge scale. Would you be surprised to find out that insects make up most of the weight? It's true! There are far more insects on Earth than any other living creature. Together, insects weigh more than all the people and other animals on the planet.

Studying Bugs

Scientists who study insects are called *entomologists*.

Identifying Insects

How do you know if an animal is an insect? Insects share some important **characteristics**. Here's how you can tell.

1. Count the legs. All adult insects have six legs.
2. Count the body parts. All adult insects have three body parts.
3. Look for wings. Most adult insects have one or two sets of wings and can fly.

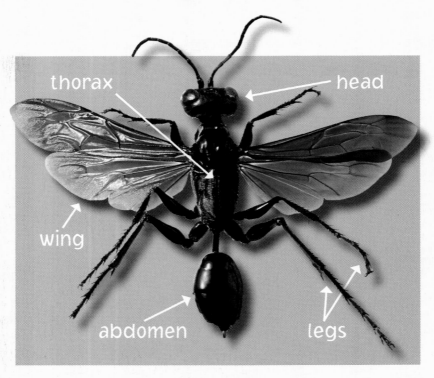

thorax

head

wing

abdomen

legs

Are Spiders Insects?

Some people think spiders are insects, but they aren't. Spiders have eight legs and two body parts. They cannot fly.

Do you collect anything? If so, you have to decide what fits in your collection by choosing things with similar characteristics. For example, you wouldn't put a football card in a baseball card collection.

Some people collect insects. They sort them into groups that are the same in some way. Sorting things into groups is called *classification*.

The members of an after-school Bug Club are telling about their insect collections. Let's listen in.

chapter 2

Helpful **Insects**

Sabrina

Sabrina is first. "Insects aren't pets, but they're not all **pests** either," she says. "I brought a helpful insect."

Sabrina sticks her finger into a jar filled with leaves. A red and black insect crawls on.

"This is a ladybug. Its real name is the *ladybird beetle*." Sabrina shows the ladybug to the other Bug Club members.

"Ladybugs eat **aphids,** a pest that harms roses," Sabrina says. "One ladybug can eat 70 aphids every day. That's over 5,000 aphids in its lifetime!"

"I'd get sick of them," calls Mabel, who has something to say about everything.

"That's because you're not a ladybug," answers Sabrina.

More of Sabrina's Favorite Helpful Insects

Honeybee

Honeybees **pollinate** flowers. They also give people honey to eat and wax to use for candles, ink, polishes, and more.

honeybee

Giant Lacewing

This large insect has lacy wings. It eats other harmful insects. The lacewing smells bad, so bug-eating birds leave it alone!

Praying Mantis

The praying mantis eats many harmful insects. It holds its front legs up, so it looks like it's praying.

praying mantis

chapter **3**

H o p p i n g **Insects**

Jacob

When it is Jacob's turn, he holds
up a picture. "This is a flea," he says.
"It's a lot smaller than it looks here.
In fact, a flea is so small that it's hard
to see."

Jacob goes on. "Fleas are good jumpers.
They have special muscles that let them
jump more than a foot. That's a long jump
for a tiny bug. In fact, the flea is the hopping
champion of the insect world!

"Fleas live on other animals. This makes the animals itchy. That's because fleas bite animals and eat their blood. Usually that doesn't hurt the animals, but fleas can transmit, or pass on, **diseases**."

"Yuck!" Mabel says.

More of Jacob's Favorite Hopping Insects

Short-Horned Grasshopper

This insect has short **antennae**. When an enemy comes near, the grasshopper uses its strong back legs to jump to safety.

Leafhopper

This big pest sucks **sap** from plants and carries disease.

It runs sideways on leaves and hops to other plants. It can fly too.

American Field Cricket

This cricket cannot fly, but its hind legs are so strong that it can hop a long way. It lives in weeds and grasses near houses.

That's a Lot of Leafhoppers

Scientists have identified more than 20,000 different kinds of leafhoppers. They think there may be more than 100,000 different kinds!

Flying **Insects**

nellie

It is Nellie's turn. "I collect flying insects!" she says. "Just look at this!"

She holds up a jar that has a colorful insect inside. "This is a monarch butterfly," Nellie explains. "Its wings are about 4 inches across! In the fall, huge groups of monarch butterflies fly south where it stays warm. Some fly more than 1,000 miles!"

"That makes me tired," Mabel yawns.

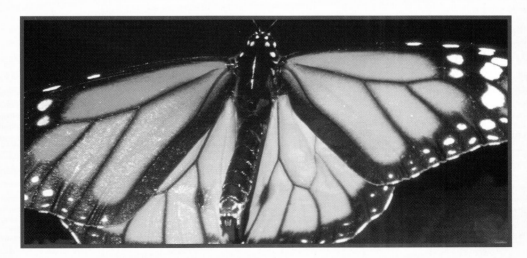

More of Nellie's Favorite Flying Insects

Twelve-Spotted Skimmer Dragonfly

This insect skims along the surface of lakes, streams, or ponds. It looks like a tiny helicopter as it hunts for food.

Yellow Jacket

This insect lives in a **colony** with a queen and workers. The female has a big stinger at the end of her body. Stay away or you might get stung!

Firefly

The firefly is a kind of beetle. It is also called the *lightning bug*. Male fireflies flash a bright light to attract females.

noisy Insects

Carlos

"My insect is the cicada," Carlos says. "It spends 17 years underground," he explains. "Some years hundreds of them crawl out in the spring. They climb into trees and shed their skin. Then they open their wings and start buzzing."

Carlos waves his arms and makes a loud, buzzing sound.

"Ouch!" Mabel says. "That hurts my ears."

"Sorry," says Carlos. "The buzzing lasts for nearly two months. But after the females lay their eggs, the cicadas die. Then it's quiet.

"One month later, the eggs hatch and **nymphs** crawl out. They dig deep into the ground, away from enemies. They'll eat sap from tree roots for the next 17 years. Then they will come out and start buzzing."

Mabel covers her ears, just in case.

More of Carlos's Favorite Noisy Insects

Katydid

Katydids live in trees, tall grasses, and weeds. Most are green, but some are brown or even pink. Katydids sing loudly at night. It sounds like they're saying, "Katy-did-did-did."

Cricket

Male crickets make a musical noise by rubbing their wings together.

Mosquito

Mosquitoes make a loud, buzzing sound. Look out when you hear it! Mosquitoes bite people and animals and suck their blood.

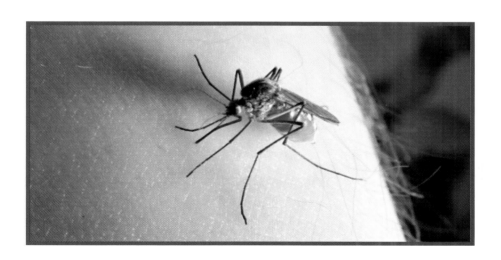

Glossary

antenna   insect body part used for smelling and touching

aphid   small insect that kills plants by sucking out their juices

characteristic   common quality shared by a group

classification   grouping by category

colony   group of creatures that lives together

disease   illness or sickness

· ·

entomologist	scientist who studies insects
nymph	name for a young insect. Nymphs look like the adult insect, but they do not have wings.
pest	creature that bothers or harms other living things
pollinate	to spread pollen from one plant to another
sap	juice of a plant

Index